RHINO SKIN

*Develop Super Tough Mental Armour
Overcome Negativity And Setbacks
With Courage And Confidence*

MARK LLEWHELLIN

Book 7 in the
Mark Llewhellin
Success and Happiness Series

DEDICATION

This book is dedicated to the love of my life, my little miracle, Léon James Llewhellin, who I love more than anyone in the world. You are kind, thoughtful, well balanced and you are already achieving great things in your life.

You are my biggest reason for having my life in order and having rhino skin in challenging times.

Words cannot describe how much I love you and how proud I am of the person you are.

GET TWO OF MARK'S BOOKS FOR FREE

Join Mark's team for information on new books along with special offers and pick up a FREE copy of Mark's 5 star reviewed books:

'The Underdog' and 'Delusions Of Grandeur.'

Details can be found at the end of this book.

TABLE OF CONTENTS

INTRODUCTION

"You have power over your mind – not outside events.
Realise this, and you will find strength."
– Marcus Aurelius

Rhino Skin

"SUBMIT, SUBMIT YOU FUCKING HONKY SPASTIC!"

I was pinned down on the floor and he was forcing pressure on my joints. I knew if my attacker put a bit more pressure on my arm, he would break it!

I have worked nine years as a bouncer. But when I was pinned down on this occasion, it wasn't by a drunk or druggie who wanted to tear me a new asshole. It was by my best friend – Des Blackwood.

I met Des when I was 16 years old when I joined the Army and went into Junior Leaders Regiment, Royal Artillery.

Des was one of the very few black recruits. And like the other two black recruits I knew, Des was as tough as nails. He didn't give a fuck what anyone thought about him and had this cool, quiet confidence, and I loved that about him.

When it came to being mentally strong, Des was a ninja master!

Sometimes Des and I used to have fights. They weren't real punching fights. They were toy, but often painful grappling fights. Des was very agile and slippery, which made it difficult for me to get the better of him.

On this occasion, I had got to the stage mentally where I wasn't screaming in pain or pleading with him to stop hurting me. Rather, I was enjoying it.

I looked at him with my eyes wide open, wildly shaking my head from side to side and laughing.

"COME ON THEN! COME ON MOTHERFUCKER... BREAK MY ARM, COME ON!"

When he heard me say that and saw how I was acting (like Jack Nicholson in 'The Shining'), he stopped putting pressure on my arm, slowly shook his head from side to side and said, "You're a crazy bastard!"

After I got to the stage of not caring if he broke my arm, he stopped and got off me.

Des would say things to me like, "look at you, you're pathetic, you're a mong. Look at you, you fucking spaz!"

This could be in the middle of a grappling match, or even if I was just walking down the corridor minding my business.

When I was in school, there were children who would say harsh words, but Des took things to a whole new level.

Of course, some things he said were highly politically incorrect. But back then it wasn't as if you could say, "hang on a minute, that's not politically correct; and if you don't stop, I'm going to my safe space."

In the Army, there was no safe space!

Des was like a black Yoda, and I was his student.

When I look back at the way he was, and how he spoke to me sometimes, I can honestly say that I'm eternally grateful.

Even though we lost touch after Junior Leaders, Des definitely toughened me up in that one year we had together. Some people may think Des took things too far, but I just classed it as training and that training has helped me throughout my life.

In the military you have to put up with a whole load of banter, but I loved it. It was extremely rare that I would let anybody get into my head in a 'banter war with words.'

In 29 Commando, there were a lot of characters. One lad was Brummie Walton. If Brummie thought you did something or said something stupid, he would stick his tongue into the bottom of his mouth in between his chin and his bottom lip.

He then made a weird noise, which I can only describe as some sort of mix between a foghorn and a sheep.

When he finished with his unique noise, he'd say… "You fucking retard!"

In the army, there weren't many limits. If somebody wanted to call you something and imply that you were a slow learner who practiced necrophilia and beastiality on the weekends, tough shit! You had to deal with it.

That sort of behaviour may appal some people reading these words, but that's just the way it was. In the army it was either adapt, or crumble! It's the same in life. Whatever comes our way, we must adapt and overcome any challenges that are thrown at us.

This book will help you develop a thick rhino-like skin. It will help you deflect criticism and rejection.

It'll give you superior mental toughness.

It can pull you out of dark times and help you achieve more success and happiness than you ever dreamed possible.

Rather than read this book like it's just another book, read it as if your life depends on the information in here, because one day it just might!

CHAPTER 1

BEAUTY IS IN THE EYE OF THE BEHOLDER

"Frankly my dear, I don't give a damn."
– Clark Gable (In 'Gone With The Wind')

Rhino Skin

On 25 October 1881, a baby boy was born in Málaga, Southern Spain.

His father – José Ruiz y Blasco, was a drawing teacher and taught him to draw pigeons by the time he was a little boy, but he mostly enjoyed drawing bulls.

When he was seven years old, he got formal art training from his father and did his first oil painting.

He was fascinated with other paintings, and other artists inspired him.

When he was only seven years old, his sister, Conchita sadly died of diphtheria.

This was devastating to the entire family, and the young boy dealt with it by losing himself in his artwork.

By the time he was 13 years old, his father felt that his son had surpassed him as an artist.

He moved to Barcelona, where his Dad took a position at the Barcelona School of Fine Arts.

Here, his Dad persuaded officials at the academy to let his son take an entrance exam for the advanced art class.

This usually took students around one month, but the boy completed it all in a week and, at only 13 years old, he was allowed into the Academy.

Fortunately, his Dad was supportive of him and sent him to one of the country's top art schools – The Real Academia de Bellas Artes de San Fernando.

Although he was at a great art school, he struggled with how he was being taught, and what he was told to paint.

This deeply troubled him, and he wanted to be his own person and do his own thing.

He soon became friends with other artists and moved to Paris, which was the centre of the art world.

The young boy, now a young man, could paint brilliant real-life looking paintings.

However, the paintings he loved painting were very obscure and strange looking.

He got criticised for this and some people thought he was wasting his talent.

Some believed the young man should follow the usual route and produce paintings popular at the time.

Once he started work on his painting, he would work for hours on end.

Sometimes he would start at 8 o'clock in the evening and work right through till the early hours of the morning and then slept in the day.

He had little money, so he covered his old canvases with new paintings. It was also reported that he burned some of his paintings to keep warm.

Between 1901 and 1904, he went through a phase where his paintings were monochromatic paintings in shades of blue and blue-green.

Many of the paintings were of gaunt looking people and looked very grim. There were a lot of people that didn't like these paintings.

However, he didn't care what other people said. He had thick rhino skin and painted them anyway.

During 1904-1906, he went through his rose period. This has a lighter tone and utilises orange and pink colours and featured lots of circus people.

He then moved to an area within the Catalan Mountains, which was a dry and lonely place, and a far cry from the hustle bustle of action-packed Paris!

Most of the houses were very square looking, which influenced his paintings, but he was also very much an artist that painted how he felt.

The young man moved in between Spain and France to work because he loved both places.

He painted controversial art with things like brothel scenes and also painted in the form of Cubism (basically anything that he was painting, ended up in a cube form with sharp edges).

When photography became popular, he was deeply upset about this and thought, 'what's the point in painting any more when reality can be captured in a photo.'

However, on the plus side of this, he wanted to be

different, and he wanted to create something different.

The young man fell in love with a beautiful woman called Eva and things were going brilliantly for him.

He decided this was the woman that he wanted to spend the rest of his life with.

However, Eva got a chronic cough and developed a fever in 1914; the doctors found out she had contracted tuberculosis.

The young man was anxious, but knew that many people survive tuberculosis, so he hoped that the love of his life would pull through.

Sadly, Eva got worse and later died.

This was another devastating loss.

The woman of his dreams had been taken from him and it ripped his heart out!

On top of that, he suffered another blow when his closest and dearest friend died in a lot of pain and discomfort from the Spanish flu.

While I write these words, we're in a nationwide lockdown

with the COVID-19 global pandemic, and although it may seem unusual to many of us, there have been many deadly diseases throughout history.

Spanish flu was reported to have killed in between 300 million to 500 million people! It is estimated that tuberculosis (at the time of writing) is the leading infectious cause of death in the world. It kills 4,109 people daily and roughly 1.5 million people every year!

Tuberculosis was responsible for one in every nine deaths in the United States in 1906. If adjusted to current population levels, it would be the equivalent of 540,000 Americans dying of tuberculosis every year.

It killed as many people as cancer and diabetes!

However, in rich countries such as the UK, USA, Germany, France and Australia etc we don't really hear about tuberculosis anymore because it's easier to treat if you're in a rich country.

At 40 years old, our painter became a father to a baby boy. He also used his son in his paintings, which documented his life. This is something that I have seen before with successful people. Two of the recent people that I was writing about also use their real life stories to write songs; they are Taylor Swift and Ed Sheeran, who both share common success traits with our painter. They are both highly prolific and produce a lot of content.

The painter then painted people and made them look like giants.

He also painted deformed looking people.

But if that was not strange enough, he started doing paintings about bestiality and mythical Minotaur's (half man and half bull) raping women.

Our artist was only 5ft 4' and had his own distinctive themes, but he always followed his heart and never listened to his critics.

Even though he had gone through a rough time, things turned out well for him.

He fell in love with another woman and his unusual paintings started to sell, and they sold for a lot.

The painter's name was Pablo Picasso!

According to Vanity Fair, when Picasso died at 91, he had produced:

1,885 paintings.

1,228 sculptures.
7,089 drawings.
150 sketchbooks.
3,222 ceramic works.
And there are reported to be 30,000 prints.

Here are some things that we can take from the Pablo Picasso story.

He:

- Picked himself up when times were tough.

- Was very focused.

- Produced a lot of work.

- Always questioned the normal way of doing things.

- Took risks.

- Created work different from the norm.

- Enjoyed being different.

- Had thick rhino skin and carried on doing what he loved, regardless of what others thought.

For me personally, many of his paintings do nothing for me. They're not the paintings I can appreciate, as I prefer bright coloured paintings with a happier look about them.

However, what I like isn't what everybody likes, and people are prepared to pay millions of pounds for Picasso's paintings.

On the 4th of May 2010, Christie's sold Pablo Picasso's Nude, Green Leaves, and Bust. It was a painting that Picasso created in a single day in 1932.

The paintings sold for $106.5 million!

On the 26th of March 2013, Pablo Picasso's Le Rêve (which looks like a deformed woman with a penis coming out of her chin) sold for $155 million!

On the 11th of May 2015, Picasso's Les Femmes (which looks like different jigsaw puzzles squashed together) sold for $179.4 million!

Picasso wasn't the only one that did things differently.

To many people, Jackson Pollock's paintings look like a three-year-old has been let loose with a paintbrush and scattered paint onto a blank canvas.

Nevertheless, Jackson Pollock's No.5, 1948, sold for $140 million and his Number 17A sold for $200 million!

And let's not even get into Mark Rothko's No. 6 (Violet, Green and Red) which sold for $186 million or Willem de Kooning's Interchange, which sold for $300 million!

The most expensive painting sold at $400 million was Leonardo da Vinci's Salvator Mundi.

The painting is of Jesus by arguably the most famous painter in history.

Even though the dollar figure is mind blowing for a painting, you can understand why it's the most expensive.

The moral of the story? Just because you're different, it doesn't mean that you're not brilliant!

So, follow your heart, put on your rhino skin, and do what you love doing.

CHAPTER 2

SHIELDS UP

*"I will not let anyone walk through my mind
with their dirty feet."*
– Gandhi

In Star Trek there is often a scene where an alien spaceship looks as if it's about to attack the USS Enterprise.

It's at this point when Captain Kirk usually says, "Shields up motherfuckers!"

Okay, maybe he doesn't say that last word, but "Shields up" is how he usually rolls in times of imminent danger.

Unless you're living on a different planet, most of us have seen movies like 'Star Trek,' 'Independence Day,' or 'Star Wars,' where the good guys, or the bad guys, put up a force-field around their spaceship to stop the enemy from damaging the ship and blowing them all to Kingdom come!

But force-fields don't just exist in science fiction books and movies.

When you think about volcanoes, it's easy to think about

the destruction they can cause. But the most significant thing about volcanoes is because they spill out radioactive lava; it proves there is a nuclear furnace deep down at the Earth's core.

Inside the Earth's core it is full of molten iron and nickel, which is always moving around deep below the Earth's surface.

It's very easy for people to think it's of no relevance to us, however if it weren't for this core below, we would all be in big trouble.

When the molten iron and nickel moves around, it creates its own magnetic field. It's believed that this magnetic field goes as far as 400,000 miles out into space, and it surrounds the Earth.

So, our planet has a force-field called the 'Earth's magnetic field,' which is also known as the 'geomagnetic field.' This magnetic field is vital to us on Earth because it deflects the deadly radiation that comes from the Sun, so it protects us from the Sun's deadly rays.

Without it, there is every chance that our planet would look something like Mars.

A magnetic field is generally invisible, but it can be seen

when the Sun flares up and sends electrically charged particles (called the solar wind) into the Earth's atmosphere.

These electrically charged particles travel at very high speeds, which cause the Aurora Borealis a.k.a. the Northern Lights or the Aurora Australis a.k.a. the Southern Lights to show up.

This magnetic field deflects 98% of the solar wind and keeps us safe here on earth.

About 2% of the Sun's UV (ultraviolet) radiation is getting through because we are being protected by our outer magnetic field, and our second shield, which we call the ozone layer, also protects us.

If 100% of the Sun's UV radiation got through to the Earth, our skin would be badly burnt in seconds. It would also break down the DNA in our healthy cells and we would all end up with myriad cancers, and, life on earth as we know it, would come to an end!

So, the safety of the Earth relies on the Earth's core to protect it from the harsh and deadly Sun in space.

As humans, we also have to protect ourselves psychologically.

This psychological force-field comes from deep inside us and protects us when we are attacked by external forces, whether it's on a mental level or a physical level. In other words, we have to create a psychological force-field around ourselves to protect ourselves from the harsh realities of life.

Just as the Earth's magnetic field is generated by the motion of molten iron alloys in its outer core, we also must be active in becoming stronger psychologically, so we too can develop a force-field in the core of us that protects us from harmful things coming from the outside.

In life, we all get attacked mentally at some point.

Someone will try to criticise you and try to tear you down, so when this happens, you need to have that mental force-field around yourself!

Some criticism can be constructive, and it can help you, but if you feel the criticism you're getting is not constructive, and is just meant to tear you down, then you need to guard your feelings from such an attack.

Some of the best ways you can guard yourself from a verbal or written attack is by feeding your mind with positive words, whether it's from:

- A close friend.

- Uplifting music.

- A supportive family member.

- Watching something inspirational.

- Reading a positive book like this one.

This will help you develop a tougher mental core.

One of my friends never fails to make me laugh because of his attitude. There are times when he's brought trouble to his doorstep that was from his own doing, which makes me laugh because he's such a character and does things that I would never do. Not that I'm perfect.

But I've also known him to be accused of some pretty horrible things that he hasn't done.

When people are criticising him, he says phrases such as "I couldn't give two fucks" or "zero fucks given."

I can't help laughing even as I'm writing these words because I find his attitude is hilarious. I also recognise that this quality is in me.

In many ways, he and I are very different people, but one thing we have in common is we both have rhino skins. We brush criticism off pretty quickly, and we both put a force-field around ourselves when someone is trying to tear us down.

Some people may look at this as an arrogant attitude to have, but if you take things to heart all the time, then you'll end up suffering a whole lot of hurt in your life. So, you've got to protect yourself from people that don't like you.

The best way to protect yourself is to avoid these people altogether, but sometimes that's just not possible. Maybe they're criticising you on social media, or maybe it's a family member that you have to see every now and again.

Ultimately you have to limit the time that you're around these people and instead mix with people who are mentally strong. People that are mentally strong, have an ability to fall into a barrel of shit and end up coming out smelling of roses.

I enjoy watching what happens in my friends life because it's like watching a real-life soap opera.

In the UK, the two biggest soap operas on TV are 'Coronation Street' and 'EastEnders.' Although the shows are popular, there's always some negative crap going on in them, so I avoid watching things like this.

I'd rather phone up my mate every now and again for five minutes just so I can amuse myself with what's going on in his life. And no matter what is happening in his life, he stays strong and doesn't let people defeat him mentally.

Some people who know him well would definitely call him a smug bastard, but that's one of the reasons he makes me laugh so much.

The point of this is, if you're going through a difficult time, then read a book like this one or listen to a friend who is strong, has gone through some tough challenges and has overcome them.

We all go through challenges, but the last person you want to learn from to make yourself stronger mentally is somebody that's mentally weak and complains all the time.

So:

- Get around strong friends who already have rhino skins.

- Put a mental force-field around yourself.

- And always remember, you have rhino skin, and nothing and nobody can break you!

CHAPTER 3

MARCH TO THE BEAT OF YOUR OWN DRUM

"The future belongs to those who believe in the beauty of their dreams."
– Eleanor Roosevelt

Sometimes people will think others are inferior because of their race, religion, sex, colour or disabilities.

When:

- Eminem started rapping; many Black people thought a White person rapping was ridiculous.

- Tiger Woods started playing golf; many White people thought a Black person playing golf was ridiculous.

- Larry Bird started playing basketball; many Black people thought he had no place on the basketball courts because he's White.

- Jackie Robinson started playing baseball; many White people thought he had no place on a baseball field because he was Black.

- Arthur Ashe was playing tennis; many Black and White people thought a Black man didn't belong on the tennis courts.

Ashe, just like the other people I've mentioned, achieved massive success in his field. He became the first Black player selected to go onto the United States Davis Cup team and won three Grand Slam singles titles, including Wimbledon.

One day I watched a programme on how a group of Indian girls started drumming. The girls had a dream of getting into a prestigious Indian drumming event called 'The Pongal Festival.'

These drums are not the drums as you or I would think of them like a rock bands drums, but a very basic type of drum they hold and play. They did it because they enjoyed playing the drums. The women also wanted to be a part of a team.

But most of all, they wanted to prove they could be as good as the men when it came to drumming.

Dalit Indian women get put into a category by many other religions in India as the lowest class of people, so they strive hard to make a name for themselves.

The word 'Dalit' comes from the Hindi word 'dalan' meaning oppressed or broken. One way that Dalit women can make a good name for themselves is by playing the drums. If they become good at playing the drums, it would give them an enormous amount of self-pride, especially if they beat some male groups.

If Dalit women are good at drums, they can compete in a competition with societies that are classed as higher than them. And if they beat them, or do well in the competition, it will bring a great amount of admiration to their society.

One girl who started drumming had a father who said he was very disappointed not to have a son.

This hurt the daughter's feelings, but rather than feel like a victim and not do anything, she decided that anything a son could do, she could also do.

The team of girls spent countless hours practising on the drums and got to a level where they became very good. This opened up a window for them and they could now enter the competition.

They were the first all-female drumming group in the history of The Pongal Festival.

Many men looked on in disgust when the women turned up at the festival with their drums. Most of the men thought the women would not do very well. They thought the women shouldn't be up there drumming because this was a man's sport.

As the women played their hearts out, something miraculous happened, people in the audience, even the men were impressed with how well they were doing. There were still a lot of negative men in the crowd because of the sexism in India.

However, these women didn't let that stop them, because they were marching to the beat of their own drum!

One of the interesting things I noticed was that the children watching didn't care whether it was men or women playing; they just wanted to hear good drumming and have a great time.

In other words, the sexism and the prejudices were handed down from generations of parents.

Against all odds, the Dalit women won the competition!

The dad that wanted a son and not a daughter came in second place with his team. However, he was happy with how well the women's team performed and was very proud of his daughter.

By winning the competition, the women inspired lots of people, which lead to others wanting to learn from them.

I always love seeing people do well in life no matter what race, religion, or gender they are. These people have shown it doesn't matter where you come from; it matters where you're going!

If anybody thinks you can't achieve your goal, then to hell with them. You have to believe in your goal, and you have to put in a lot of work and effort to make your goal a reality!

Regardless of opinions, you have to march to the beat of your own drum and by doing this you will inspire lots of other people to succeed.

So, no matter what race, religion, colour or gender you are, put on your rhino skin, and march to the beat of your own drum!

CHAPTER 4

YOU CAN'T PLEASE EVERYONE

"Do what you feel in your heart to be right, for you will be criticised anyway."

– Eleanor Roosevelt

When I wanted to sell my first book, I decided that the best way to do it would be to get donations from a website called 'Go Fund Me.' As I got more experienced as an author, I found out that this wasn't the best way to sell books. However, it gave me a start.

I told people if they made a donation of £10 or more, I would give them a signed copy of my paperback book 'The Underdog.'

Just before I published my second book 'Delusions Of Grandeur' I wanted to send advance copies to the fan base I had already built up.

This loyal fan base became known as my 'Advance Reader Copy Team' and they would duly get a copy of the e-book free before the publishing date. They then gave some constructive criticism and told me what they thought about the book, as well as identifying any grammar or typing errors that had bypassed the proofreading.

I went onto Facebook and I asked if anyone wanted to be part of my Advanced Copy Reader Team for my next book.

I had an incredible response, and over 100 people came onboard asking if they could be part of the team of advanced readers (5 weeks later this number grew to over 1,300 people).

One person in the comment section put something slightly different.

His message said words to the effect of:

"I am not helping Mark Llewhellin anymore, I have given him £20 for his first book and it hasn't arrived, I'm not satisfied."

Somehow this guy had slipped through the net and I didn't send him a book, which was a totally unintentional oversight!

But rather than inbox me asking when he will get his book, he decided to publicly slander me on Facebook. When I checked to see if he had sent me any inbox messages, there were none.

He didn't ask me where his book was, in fact he didn't

even send me his address, so there was no way I could have posted the book to him anyway. Rather, he thought he would tell the world about how much of a bastard I was.

Of course, some of my friends saw his comment on Facebook and jumped to my defence. Not wanting to get involved with any silly little arguments, I simply deleted all the comments.

To have a successful business, and an easier life, it's generally better to keep people happy. So, I messaged the guy, apologised to him for not sending his book, and offered to send his paperback book to him.

In the meantime, I sent him a free audiobook version while he was waiting for his paperback.

If you mess up and you know that you're in the wrong, which I was (by not sending the book to him straight away), I always feel it's a good idea to apologise and to also give the person something else as a sign of good will.

He then sent me a private inbox message and asked me why I had taken his comment off Facebook. The guy knew other people had commented on it, but he couldn't see the comments because I already deleted them.

He told me he was outraged, and he wasn't happy with the way this situation was going. The guy basically went into 'victim mode,' got on his high horse, and had a go at me via my inbox.

He told me he didn't want the paperback copy anymore, and that he just wanted a refund. So, he got a free audiobook, and I also gave him a full refund.

So, how bad did I feel about this whole situation?

Well, if you look at the cover of the book you're reading, you can probably guess how bad I felt.

Some people may think that this is an arrogant way of looking at things, but when you make a mistake, all you can do is apologise for what you've done. Try to rectify the situation and do your best to make the person happy.

If they're still upset, there is nothing more you can do. You've done everything you can, and if they're still not happy and want to tear you a new asshole, that's just the way things go. You simply can't have people ruining your day because of petty things.

Forgetting to send him his book on time was hardly the crime of the century, but he blew it up out of all proportion.

I had made the same mistake of not posting a book to 2 other people, but rather than throw their teddy in the corner, they said, "do you know when I'll get my copy of The Underdog?" Those two situations were resolved with no dramas because they handled it maturely.

As for the keyboard warrior, he'll probably move on to the next person and unnecessarily struggle through life. A fact of life is that some people are just going to criticise you.

It doesn't matter if you're the nicest person in the world you will at some point in your life attract some unnecessary negativity from some people.

In early 2020 a girlfriend that I used to go out with, criticised lots of little things that I did. She told me I was the nicest guy she'd ever been with, but for her own reasons, she was nitpicking at me all the time.

Ironically, at the start of the relationship, I was this perfect person in her eyes. However, I could see she was going through troubled times and she tried to dampen down my positivity and enthusiasm for life.

Maybe you once had a partner that criticised you too?

Michael Jordan, who was one of, if not the greatest basketball player of all time famously said,

"My fame, it was good at the beginning, people talk about you in a positive way, it's great to hear those comments. But now that you are on a pedestal, it's not just the positive talking that you're hearing. Some people take shots at you."

When Michael Jordan was getting criticised for losing games, he would use that criticism as fuel to spur him on. He developed a 'fuck you' attitude and ended up winning more games. And that's exactly what you can do.

With negative people just:

- Put on your rhino skin.

- Smile.

- Be positive.

- Walk around like you haven't got a fucking care in the world.

- Wish them all the best.

- And don't give two fucks

Some people will hate you even more, but that's their problem.

Whatever you do, make sure they don't see they've got to you. Some people that have criticised you may apologise but many people will get a kick out of seeing you pissed off! Because boy oh boy do they really want to see you crash and burn!

Don't give them an inch, you're a champion!

You're a winner!

And there's nothing they can do to make you unhappy, because you've got rhino skin, you're too strong for them, and you're above all of that shit!

Rhino Skin

CHAPTER 5

ELECTRICAL ENTHUSIASM

"Try, for who knows what is possible."
– Michael Faraday

On the 22nd September 1791, a little boy by the name of Michael was born in Newington Butts, which is now an area known as Elephant and Castle in London, England.

He wasn't very well educated, and many people thought he'd be a failure in life, and he wouldn't amount to anything. Even though he wasn't formally educated, he was obsessed with learning new things and read everything he could to gain more knowledge.

Like many successful people, Michael spent a lot of his free time self-educating.

He was the type of person who didn't wait around to be given something. If he wanted to do something or find out something, he would act towards making it a reality.

Michael was the son of a blacksmith who had a lot of health challenges and times were very tough, not only with his father's poor health but also with the lack of money that came into the household. However, they qualified for help from the government, which came in the form of one extra loaf of bread a week.

Although the extra loaf of bread was a help, it didn't go very far, as there were six people in Michael's family, so life wasn't easy, and he would sometimes go to bed hungry.

Even though we may look at one loaf of bread a week as not much support from the government, it is still far more than many other people around the world get!

Michael's first job was at 13, when he became a bookbinders apprentice.

Being a bookbinder was far from Michael's dream, but he knew it would bring in more cash for his family, so they could eat and live, and he also read many of the books that came into the shop. It was here where he developed an interest in science. The things that he most loved reading about were force and energy.

Michael attended lectures and listened to speakers who were at the cutting edge of science.

One customer that went to Michael's bookbinding shop was a man by the name of William Dance. Dance knew that Michael was extremely interested in learning new things in science.

He also liked Michael, as Michael was kind, helpful, and very enthusiastic when people came into the shop.

Dance was one founder of the Royal Philharmonic Society and was extremely well connected. In 1812, he gave Michael one of four tickets to four lectures.

Little did Michael know at the time; these four lectures would completely change his life!

Highly educated people attended the lectures and some of them looked down on him, as he was clearly from a lower class with a poor educational background. However, Michael didn't let this deter him because he had rhino skin. And no matter what criticism he received, he remained relentless in pursuing his dreams.

He knew it didn't matter where someone starts off from; it just mattered where they were going!

The man speaking at the lecture was a Cornish chemist and inventor named Sir Humphry Davy, who was the first person to isolate a series of elements such as sodium, potassium, calcium, barium, strontium, and magnesium.

He discovered the elemental nature of iodine and chlorine.

Sir Humphry invented a new field of electrochemistry.

He also experimented with nitrous oxide and nicknamed it laughing gas.

If you've seen any of the 'Fast and Furious' movies; or you are a racing enthusiast, I'm sure you would've heard of it called by its other name... 'nitrous!'

Davy wrote about the potential of nitrous oxide as an anaesthetic for relieving pain during surgery.

He invented the 'Davy' lamp, which was a safety lamp and used in flammable atmospheres such as coal mines that contained methane and other flammable gases.

It reduced the risk of explosions in coal mines and saved many lives!

The Davy lamp was an early form of lightbulb and variants of it have been used many times for the torch at the Olympic Games.

Sir Humphry Davy became an inspirational figure to Michael, just as Benjamin Thompson (a physicist and inventor whose challenges established physical theory and revolutionised thermodynamics) was an inspirational figure to Sir Humphry.

The more Michael got around high achievers in the world of science, the more inspired he was, which resulted with him wanting to push his own boundaries and achieve great things. Even though Michael's status was well below these people, he had rhino skin and he dreamed that one day he would have significant breakthroughs of his own and he could be looked upon as an equal.

Michael took highly detailed notes at Sir Humphry's lectures. He worked day and night to come up with an impressive book which he bound together and presented it to Sir Humphry.

Sir Humphry was impressed with Michael's book and was interested in what path Michael was going to take in life.

However, Davy had little initial interest in helping Michael pursue his dream of science and Michael returned to his day job.

Michael stayed humble, he used his people skills, and eventually, through his enthusiasm, tenacity and rhino-thick skin, Sir Humphry took him under his wing, and he became Sir Humphry's laboratory assistant.

From that point on, Michael would soak up every bit of knowledge that Sir Humphry would give to him.

Some people questioned why a man of Sir Humphry's status would work with Michael because of his poor background. Maybe this was because Sir Humphry himself also came from a similar background. But it was most likely because he could see potential in Michael. He loved that Michael was such a kind and enthusiastic person.

The battery had just been invented and electricity excited scientists.

The trouble was, nobody could work out exactly what electricity was!

Sir Humphry and his team discovered that when you put a magnetic compass next to an electric current, it would move the compass.

At the time, everyone believed that electricity flows through a wire.

However, Michael suggested that there was a possibility that if electricity was flowing through wire, then there must also be invisible lines of force outside of the electric wire, which was moving the magnetic compass.

Some prominent scientists thought that this was a ridiculous suggestion.

However, there were those that didn't totally dismiss it. This was because they couldn't understand why the compass was moving when it was near the wire with electricity flowing through it.

Despite the criticism, Michael became obsessed with the magnetic compass and electricity.

Then one day Michael conducted a revolutionary experiment:

He filled a glass with mercury, which is an excellent conductor. Then Michael put a magnet at the bottom of the glass and suspended a wire from above, which went into the glass. An external battery then sent a current to the wire that was hanging into the glass, and because the magnet was placed at the bottom of the glass, the magnetic field made the wire spin.

Many people didn't know it, but what Michael had created lead to one of the biggest inventions of the century… the invention of the electric motor!

Just to give you a heads up on how significant the electric motor is, here are some inventions that work by using an electric motor: washing machine, tumble dryers, vacuum cleaners, fans, air conditioner, refrigerator, freezers, CD drives, hair dryers, can openers, electric razors, hair trimmers, electric knives, beard trimmers, electric forklift, subway trains, electric cars, golf carts, segways, computer CPU, laptop, grinder, toys, garage opener, electric saw, electric drill, windscreen wipers, trains, electric cars and many more things.

Michael invented an early form of the Bunsen burner.

He discovered chemical substances such as benzene and liquefied gases like chlorine and was also the first to report on what later came to be called 'metallic nanoparticles.'

When you were a child, did you ever play with balloons? Or have you ever seen how happy a young child is when they're playing with a balloon at a party? You can thank Michael for that happiness because he invented the rubber balloon in 1824.

Michael was also responsible for the 'Faraday Cage.' You may or may not have heard of the Faraday Cage, but you have certainly benefited from it!

Somebody can stand inside a Faraday Cage and be protected from electricity outside the cage.

This is because it collects and distributes electrostatic charges around the outside of the cage, and that protects whatever, or whoever, is in it.

Most of us have never been inside an old Faraday Cage, but you and I have been into things that use Faraday Cages; possibly the two best examples of these are cars and planes. Airlines and car manufacturers want to protect people driving or flying if their vehicle gets hit by a bolt of lightning. The Faraday Cage is built into the vehicle so you are more protected.

His Faraday Cage is also a vital part of your microwave because it keeps most of the microwave radiation on the inside.

The list of Michael's achievements goes on and on.

Here are some things that we can learn from Michael's story.

- If you are having or have had financial challenges, you're not alone.

- If you are doing a job that isn't your dream job, look for the benefits it can give you while you make moves to get into your dream job.

- Be kind.

- It doesn't matter what your formal education is, you can learn more if you put the time and effort in yourself.

- Don't take it to heart if people look down on you.

- Use people's negativity as an inspirational tool and leave them in your wake.

- Learn how to become a great networker.

- Be humble and willing to learn.

- Get around inspirational people.

- Read books you enjoy and that inspire you because they will help you become happier and more successful.

- Have big dreams.

- Never give in.

- Be enthusiastic, you will not only learn more, but you will attract more people that will want to help you.

Michael was offered a knighthood from the Queen but declined it. He was also asked to work for the government to develop chemical weapons, but turned that down too. Michael was known as a kind soul that wanted to help other people and make their lives better.

Michael's full name is Michael Faraday!

Despite his tough beginnings, Michael Faraday changed the world for the better and became one of the most important science figures in history!

Faraday was a genius in every sense of the word.

However, his genius would never have been recognised if he didn't have rhino skin to keep him going through all the setbacks.

Although Michael Faraday had many successes, he also had many failures. But nobody remembers him for his failures, and no one will remember you for your failures as long as you keep going through your setbacks.

So put on your rhino skin, be enthusiastic, stay strong, and keep going until you reach your goals!

Rhino Skin

62

CHAPTER 6

DEFLECT REJECTION

"You have losses you never thought you'd experience. You have rejection. You learn how to deal with that and how to get up the next day and go on."
– Taylor Swift

Rhino Skin

If you want to be successful at certain things, you will experience rejection somewhere along the way.

Many people feel down when they constantly get rejected, but if your dream is big, you may have to go through the numbers to achieve your goal.

Sometimes it's hard to know if your approach is the right approach. You could use the wrong words or technique, so sometimes you just have to adjust. You should get into the mindset of welcoming rejection because every rejection is closer to you succeeding.

Over the years, I've been turned down by many of the girls that I've asked out. This isn't a badge of honour because everyone wants to be the man or the lady who everyone adores.

No one really wants to tell people about their failings with the opposite sex because we all like to believe that we're special and anyone and everyone should date us. But this isn't always the case.

People who are very good looking or kind or rich or have a superb physique get turned down.

Of course, having some of those things going for you helps a lot. But if you have got none of them, you may just have to ask more people out. You might get turned down more, but eventually you'll hit a home run.

It doesn't matter who you are, you're going to get rejection in your life. Simply look at everything as a numbers game. Business, opportunities, fitness or whatever else it is you want; you must be ACTIVE and KEEP GOING!

Sam Walton, the founder of supermarket giant 'Walmart' became so successful because he had rhino skin and could go from failure to failure without losing his enthusiasm.

Before he was married, Sir Michael Caine asked a girl out, and she rejected him nine times.

He asked her one more time and thought to himself, "If she doesn't go out with me now then that's it, I'm not going to ask her ever again."

On the 10th time he asked her out, she said yes, and they

have been married for 46 years at the time of writing.

When somebody has a new idea and another person shits all over it, the person with the idea can often get discouraged. Especially if the critic is respected.

When you know you haven't got someone's support, it may dishearten you at first. However, never let it stop you from pursuing your goal if your goal is something you strongly believe in.

The day before I wrote these words, I was talking to a well-respected publishing agent about a book idea that a friend and I are working on.

He didn't like the idea and thought it wouldn't work. This was slightly disappointing, but I never let it bother me. In fact, I just used it as motivation to drive the project forward and succeed.

I think the idea is great. My friend and co-author thinks it's a great idea, as does another 'Sunday Times' Bestselling author friend.

Will that book be successful? The truth of it is you never know. You can believe that something will work, but only time will tell. You can only do what you feel is right and follow your heart.

One of the biggest mistakes a new author makes is they get all precious and lovey-dovey about a certain book.

Not me!

Yes, there are some books that I may like more than others, but I don't treat that book as my 'precious baby.'

And if anybody doesn't like what I've written, they're already behind because I've moved onto the next book.

I may glance at a negative review about one of my books, but that's all it is, a glance. Nothing more, nothing less!

It's the same with the comments on YouTube for some of my interviews. As with the books, most of the comments are overwhelmingly positive. When I read a negative one, I just use it to motivate me.

In 2020, I produced a lot more books. In July I published one book. In August I published two books, and in October I smashed out another two books.

If I had only produced one book that year and sat around waiting for comments, money or anything else, then a negative comment may have affected me more.

And it wasn't until I published six books that things

started to pick up for me. What if I'd have looked at some negative reviews and given up after my fifth book?

When you're busy, you haven't got much time to be affected by negative comments from people.

It's like sitting on a high-speed train, and somebody standing on the side of the track shouts… "hey asshole!"

It's a case of, "yeah, cheers for that, I've already moved on."

So put that rhino skin on, keep moving, use rejection to motivate you and know that success is a numbers game!

Rhino Skin

CHAPTER 7

DON'T LET PEOPLE TIE YOU UP IN KNOTS

"If you can't tolerate critics, don't do anything new or interesting."
– Jeff Bezos

Erika, a wife and the mother of two teenage boys, had been working at the BBC in London and was going through a midlife crisis.

She read a 'Twilight' book, was inspired by it, and wrote her own novel without an outline.

An outline is the plan of a fiction book and usually includes the structure, characters, plot and the scenes.

Many authors feel it's always best to write with an outline, but Erika did her own thing.

She also wrote on her Blackberry phone on her way to work and transferred it onto a computer at a later stage. Again, writing on a phone would also be frowned upon by many authors. But Erika didn't care.

Despite her different way of doing things, she became extremely successful.

Erika is best known for her pen name E. L. James and even better known for her books… 'Fifty Shades of Grey!'

When I looked on Amazon UK, the reviews were:
58% 5-star rating.
10% 4-star rating.
11% 3-star rating.
7% 2-star rating.
And 15% 1-star rating.
That's out of a colossal 46,099 reviews.

On Amazon.com, the reviews were:
58% 5-star reviews.
11% 4-star reviews.
9% 3-star reviews.
7% 2-star reviews.
And 15% 1-star reviews.
This is out of a staggering 52,037 reviews!

Here are some Amazon reviews from people:

"I can't take it anymore. This has to be the most appallingly atrocious writing I've ever seen in a major release."

"If I wrote like that, I'd use a pseudonym too."

"What I find terribly depressing is that this is a runaway bestseller and the movie rights are expected to sell for up to 5 million."

"50 Shades is a sad joke, puny in plot."

"S&M for dummies."

"E.L. hasn't got any talent."

"Dull and poorly written."

One very bitter reviewer sounded as if she herself is also an author.

In fact, when I did a search on her, I found that there was an author by the same name who had a book out about origami. As interesting as folding bits of paper might be for some, sex is a much hotter topic for most people.

When Salman Rushdie commented on Erika's book he said, "he had never read anything so badly written that got published."

It's amusing that Rushdie said that. When he wrote his book 'The Satanic Verses' there were people all over the world who wanted him dead and he had to be put under police protection.

Some people publicly burned his book, and it sparked

violence around the world. People were so upset that certain bookstores were firebombed.

Now it's one thing to get a one-star review and a lot of criticism for your book. However, to have people want to kill you because of what you wrote takes things to a whole new level.

For me, I'm always happy for someone that does well.

When I see another author doing well, it inspires me to keep on writing my material.

Personally, I love Erika's story and how she became successful.

When Erika was interviewed by ABC she was asked, "Did you ever imagine this would take off the way it has?"

Her reply was, "Never, ever, ever, ever."

Fifty Shades of Grey was on the New York Times bestseller list for 138 weeks. Combined with her other two books in the series, her books sold at a rate of 2 books a second at one point. It became the fastest selling paperback of all time and was translated into 51 languages.

In 2012, she won Publishers Weekly Publishing Person of the Year, National Book Award, Popular Fiction Book of the Year, and National Book Award Book of the Year.

In August 2013, she hit the Number 1 spot of highest earning authors with sales of her trilogy and the film cash (an estimated total of $95 million).

According to Wikipedia, the combined novels have sold over 125 million copies worldwide. In 2012, Time magazine named her one of The World's 100 Most Influential People.

What I loved most about Erika when I watched her interviews, was that she came across as just a nice, sincere, down-to-earth person.

So no matter who you are, how nice you are or how much other people love what you do… Some people will criticise you.

Don't let that discourage you. Stay strong and charge forward!

Rhino Skin

CHAPTER 8

TAKE YOUR POWER BACK

"Conquering others takes force. Conquering yourself is true strength."
– Lao-Tzu

Rhino Skin

"He's taken my power!"

These were the words a friend of mine said when she was describing her ex-boyfriend.

Even though they were split up, she believed he had some sort of psychological control over her.

He belittled her and mentally bullied her until she was reduced to a wreck of a person.

She believed him when he told her she was useless and pathetic. And because of this, she had lost all of her confidence.

She now drank every day and without realising it, she became an alcoholic.

Psychological evaluations followed, and the social services came in because she struggled to take care of herself and her children. This behaviour put years on her life and she looked beaten down.

By indulging in this destructive behaviour, it also didn't make her as attractive to men. She had let herself go with a, "I'm worthless, and I don't give a shit anymore" attitude.

The reality was, she was a beautiful girl with a kind heart.

Before she hit the self-destruct button, most men were attracted to her.

But now, she believed she was worthless and moulded herself into her ex-boyfriend's evaluation of her.

When she told me that her ex-boyfriend had taken her power, I strongly replied, "that's bullshit! **Nobody can take your power away from you unless you give it to them!**"

So it's important to be around people that build you up and are supportive of you. When somebody is constantly belittling you, it can be an uphill battle.

Have you ever come across someone that doesn't like you?

Or somebody that belittles you either in front of you, or

behind your back?

There is a saying that goes, the 'best revenge is success.' It's a good saying, but in reality, the best revenge isn't success, it's happiness.

Even if you succeeded 99% of the time, and you have everything that you ever dreamed of; if you don't have happiness, what use is it?

Some people that don't like you will want to have some sort of psychological power over you if they can.

However, when you're happy, it takes their power over you away!

There will be people out there that have fucked you over. They may have said nasty things about you or done nasty things to you.

They want to see your life go down in flames.

Being successful is pretty cool, and it will probably wind some of your haters up.

However, being happy is far more powerful. But if you can be both happy and successful, which you can, even better!

When you're successful, happy, and mentally secure, your critics know they have no power over you.

Many haters will let go of their resentment for you. If they don't, it'll make their lives worse.

Living with hate for others isn't a healthy thing to do!

When you walk around with a 'happy-go-lucky I don't give a fuck attitude' it can upset some of your critics. That's their problem, not yours.

On the flip side, when you walk around with a happy-go-lucky attitude, many people will respect you and like you even more.

More importantly, you will like yourself more.

When people know there is nothing they can do to upset you, you have taken their power away from them and claimed your own power back!

When bullies or haters have upset you, don't let them know they've got to you. If you do, it often encourages them to be nastier. They'll think you're weak, and they know they've got power over you.

Be like a poker player; don't show them your hand.

If it's someone who genuinely cares about you, but has upset you, that's different.

Often, it's a good thing to show them your hand and tell them how you feel; doing that can clear the air.

They may sympathise with you and realise they've been too harsh and back off. If they really care about you and you care about them, it can be best to talk about your feelings. By doing this, the situation can often be resolved.

All situations are unique, and every person is different. So there is no one way to do things. How you handle any situation will have to be left to your good judgement.

Has somebody said unpleasant things to you and you believed those things?

Is there somebody out there that 'you' are holding resentment towards?

If you answered yes to any of those questions, they have power over you. Realise what is happening and take your power back.

Ultimately, get a grip of your shit and keep moving forward!

Never let anybody take your power. You're not a doormat. You don't let people walk over you. You haven't got time for any of that shit. You're too strong and too powerful!

Remember, you're a wild and free 5,000 lb thick-skinned rhino and a rhino doesn't give two fucks, because it knows how powerful it is.

So take your power back, keep smiling, and charge forward!

CHAPTER 9

THE MAGIC OF HAVING A RHINO SKIN

"You have to surround yourself with really good people and have a very thick skin."
– Cindy Margolis

One day, a Father was taking his two daughters out to play.

He took them to a park with a merry-go-round and sat there on the bench watching his children.

The Father thought to himself, 'There should be some sort of amusement park where the children and the parents could all have fun together, rather than just the parents watch the children.'

He wanted to create a small amusement park in a playground next to where he worked.

However, the local Council thought that a carnival atmosphere would come into the city. They didn't like it, so they rejected his plans.

In 1952, he formed a new company called WED Enterprises from his initials and before they secured funding, concept work began on a theme park he wanted to open.

He needed ideas for the amusement park, so he asked the people from his animation company to help him because they were big thinkers, creative and thought outside the box.

The young Father brought in architects and art directors to help him make his dream a reality.

He later called this group 'imagineers.'

The Father always encouraged his people to push the boundaries with their imagination and creativity and wanted them to take risks.

He looked for a location and came across the small town of Anaheim, Southern California, which is roughly 30 miles southeast of Los Angeles.

It has glorious weather, and the land was a lot more affordable than many other locations in Southern California.

Back then, there was no freeway to get to Anaheim, it was just full of farmland. Most people thought he was crazy for wanting to put an amusement park in the middle of nowhere!

Some of the key questions that were asked were:

- What if people can't afford it?

- What if it's too far away for people to travel to?

He didn't care what people thought because this Father had rhino skin.

During World War II, his company was hard hit, and he suffered huge financial losses. Banks refused to invest in him and his amusement park dream. They thought it was all pie in the sky and totally unrealistic.

However, he had super tough rhino skin and kept asking investors to back him.

He was a master of convincing himself that his dream would work, and just as importantly, he was a master of convincing people his dream would become a reality.

This rhino skinned go-getter's name was Walt Disney!

TV was new back then, and Walt and his brother Roy saw an opportunity.

With a map of the proposed amusement park, Roy proposed to produce a weekly TV show for the once struggling ABC network, in exchange for $5 million which would fund the park.

In 1954, Walt Disney went on TV and told the American people about his latest dream, which was the amusement park. He had planned different themes in the park:

- Fantasyland.
- Tomorrowland.
- Adventureland.
  and
- Frontierland.

His goal was to create an amusement park full of fun, knowledge and happiness.

When constructing the park, they didn't have the money to buy the plants and trees, so they came up with a clever idea and put an advert in the paper.

The advert told people, if they had a tree they didn't want, the Disney team would pick it up and put it into the park. The idea was a tremendous success.

It's very easy to look at somebody like Walt Disney and think to ourselves, how lucky he was. He was rich, and he had so much going for him.

However, he was worried, and couldn't help thinking about what would happen if the park failed.

He thought:

- Are the attractions good enough?

- Is the park safe enough?

- Will people get hurt?

- If the park fails, people will lose their jobs and it will affect them negatively.

- About when the rain flooded many areas of the new park and the problems that caused.

- It was difficult to take the criticism from the people that doubted his dream.

- About money, because he borrowed lots of money and worried about it.

The day the park first opened he had spent over $17 million, which was over three times the original budget!

On the 17th July 1955, Disneyland open to the public.

There was a massive turnout for it, and 22 cameras from across America captured the event to broadcast to the news channels.

A staggering 83 million people watched on their living room TVs.

Things weren't going as good as Disney hoped because when the park opened, the press slated it and called it a nightmare!

Here are some things that went wrong when Disneyland opened:

- There were vast amounts of counterfeit tickets, which got people in the park and made it go three times over its capacity.

- There were a lot of electrical failures on the rides.

- The vending machines run out of stock and the employees were completely overwhelmed and struggled to cope.

- People weren't waiting in line properly to go on the attractions. They were jumping over the fence and causing mayhem.

- The teacup rides were falling apart, so they had to bring in the welders.

- When people went on the Dumbo ride, it took them up in the air but didn't come back down to the ground. The staff ended up taking people off the ride from ladders.

- They had gas leaks, and the Mark Twain Paddle Steamer that people went on nearly sank.

Regardless of the problems, Walt had rhino thick skin, and never gave up!

People had never seen or experienced anything quite like it, and within only two months over 1 million people visited the park.

Walt Disney always reinvested profits to improve Disneyland. His team was always pushing boundaries.

They came up with new inventions, including the Matterhorn Bobsleds, which was the first rollercoaster of its kind in the world.

When they created the monorail, the U.S. Vice President –

Richard Nixon opened it.

Disney knew that the success of the park was hugely down to marketing, TV and media exposure.

One of the major focuses of the park was for it to have a lot of kinetics. There had to be something in motion all the time. Whether you're riding on it, or watching it, there was always something moving.

Disney and his team also came up with 'Project X.' The goal of this project was to create another theme park.

They looked for a location with:

- Wonderful weather all year.

- Reasonably priced land.

- Lots of tourists.

They chose Florida and bought 27,000 acres, which is a similar size to San Francisco.

Walt was incredibly excited about what the future held for him; however, he was about to be hit with a devastating blow!

Walt Disney sadly developed lung cancer and knew that his time was short.

With this news, he encouraged his brother Roy to fulfil the dreams that he had, especially his dream of Disney World in Florida.

The same year England won the Football World Cup in 1966, Walt Disney sadly passed.

He was only 65 years old.

Eric Sevareid – a CBS news reader said of Walt's passing, "While there is very little grown-up in a child, there is a child in every grown-up. He probably did as much to heal or soothe troubled human souls as all of the psychiatrists in the world."

Walt Disney's vision and rhino thick skin created some of the best theme parks in the world.

His movies are loved by every generation, and he has won more Academy Awards than anyone in history. His record stands at 22 Oscars.

Walt Disney touched the lives of billions of people. His legacy carries on to this day, and without his rhino skin, none of it would've happened!

Rhino Skin

CHAPTER 10

FIGHTING WITH YOUR FAMILY

"If you end up with a boring, miserable life because you listened to your Mom, your Dad, your teacher, your priest, or some guy on television telling you how to do your shit, then you deserve it."
– Frank Zappa

Rhino Skin

Have you ever disagreed with any of your family?

If you've always got on with every member of your family, then you are a very lucky and unique individual.

However, if you're like most of us, then you may have clashed with family members in the past.

It could be a: Mother, Brother, Sister, Father, Cousin, Grandparent, Grandchild, Son or Daughter.

Heck, in today's society, you could even have a trans-neutral family member. Fine by me; each to their own.

One of the biggest critics that I have is my Mum.

If you've read my book 'Man The F*ck Up,' then you know the person I call my Mum is my Auntie who brought me up after my biological Mum killed herself.

Don't get me wrong here, I love her dearly and I am so grateful for everything she's done for me.

Most of the time we get on well, but every now and again she will want to tell me what to do.

Even though I know she loves me, she can be relentless at criticising me.

Amazingly, at 47 years old I'm still treated as incompetent sometimes and there isn't much I do that doesn't warrant a correction from her.

Whether it be her telling me what I'm doing wrong or whether it's telling someone else about my shortcomings.

I know she loves me and she cares about me, but family members invariably have an opinion about you.

If you take a left turn, they may suggest you take a right turn. It's almost like they're playing devil's advocate and they constantly suggest the opposite to what you're doing.

Some people will look for the negative in everything you do. Even if you think you're doing well by most people's standards, they will still verbally run you down.

When you're related to negative people at your workplace,

it's more difficult to cut them out of your life.

With family, you may love them, and they may love you, but you have to take a break from the abuse that comes out of their mouth.

Some people never take control of the situation. They distance themselves and stop looking for solutions. In the most extreme cases, they take their own lives.

My Mum is at her worst with belittling me when I'm with my son Léon.

I've always found looking after Léon a joy.

It's extremely rare I have to correct his behaviour because he's a wonderful, kind, and polite little boy.

Things like getting Léon food, making sure he has the right clothes, and keeping him safe are the basics of parenting and I find them very easy to do.

Sadly, this doesn't stop my Mum from talking to me in a condescending way and feeling she has to 'tell' me or Léon what to do all the time.

One day she said, "I really get on your nerves sometimes don't I?"

I laughed and said to her, "anyone I know, would find it challenging when someone is constantly 'telling,' (not asking them) to do something and talking down to them. It's extremely rude."

If I do something brilliant, there is more chance of me finding a one ended stick, than there is of her praising me for something.

My friend Paul Hughes had bid for a spot for a private kicking session with British Lions and Welsh rugby player Lee Halfpenny.

Of course, these sorts of things can be a once-in-a-lifetime thing.

It's not every day parents are in a position where their son can go on private kicking sessions with one of the best in the business.

When I told my Mum I will be taking Léon on a private kicking session with Lee, she wasn't impressed.

The only thing that she said is, "he's not going to be up late is he?"

It was irrelevant to her that Léon had this fantastic opportunity.

Rather than support what Léon was doing, she only wanted to criticise me.

My Mum always looks at the negative aspects of life and is very pessimistic about most things.

Even though she is aware of my feelings, she has the closed mindset of, 'well I'm older than you, I'm stuck in my ways and I'll carry on being like this.'

Even into her 80s, she doesn't realise that she could live a much happier life if she focused on the good in people and not what she perceives to be negative.

My Mum brought me up and I can never repay her for that.

But fortunately I have taken my own path in life and because of that reason; I love my life and now live the life of my dreams.

Some people may not think that my life is that great, but I know I've come a long way and I never expected to achieve even 10% of what I have achieved in my life.

Maybe there are some things that you have achieved and you are proud of.

You might beat yourself up because you don't feel you've achieved what you wanted to achieve.

Maybe a family member isn't proud of what you've done with your life.

It's important that you tell yourself that you have done well in life.

Never underestimate your achievements and never compare yourself to others.

So put your rhino skin on, grow some rhino balls and 'do what YOU want to do' with YOUR life!

CHAPTER 11

FAR OUT THINKING ATTRACTS CRITICS

"Think little goals and expect little achievements. Think big goals and win big success."
– David Joseph Schwartz

Rhino Skin

If you wish to accomplish big things in your life, you've got to go somewhere you've never been before. This could be:

- Mentally
  and
- Physically.

To accomplish something different, you need to form different habits.

When people come up with an original idea or they choose to change who they are for the better, they often come up against criticism.

In the 19th century, German philosopher Arthur Schopenhauer said that all truth goes through three phases:

1. Ridiculed.

2.   Violently opposed.

3.   Accepted as being self evident.

No matter what you choose to do, some individuals will not accept your dream or your beliefs.

A common phrase used is, "you're biting off more than you can chew." But any enormous accomplishment has been achieved by individuals who have bitten off more than they can chew.

It takes courage because they may look an idiot in the presence of their friends and family, but if you never take risks, you'll never achieve great things in your life.

There will be individuals who say, "you need to be realistic."

However, everything you see in front of you was once someone's dream and before it was created it was once looked upon as impossible or unrealistic.

What's the worst that can happen if you screw up?

You may look foolish to some individuals, but at least you had the courage to try.

One person who was ridiculed was a young astrophysicist by the name of Eugene Parker.

He believed he had discovered the solar wind, which are streams of electrically charged nuclear particles that are blasted out from the Sun in every direction.

In the 1950s, Parker's ideas were so revolutionary, many experts thought he'd lost his marbles!

Parker went through all the three stages, but in the end, he had the last laugh as people accepted his theory to be true.

With going places people have never gone before, the team at NASA (National Aeronautics and Space Administration) are right at the top end of the spectrum!

The year at the time of writing is 2020; but 60 years before these words were written, NASA had a dream of sending a space probe with a mission. That mission was to get very close to the Sun so the exploration would pick up vital data about the activities on the Sun.

Spacecraft had been sent to the major regions of the solar system before, but had yet to go into the centre of the solar system. In other words, to the Sun.

The Delta Heavy rocket had the task of launching the

probe and getting it as close as possible to the Sun. The Sun is approximately 19 million miles away from the Earth.

Here are some other interesting statistics about the Sun:

- The heat from its core is 27 million degrees Fahrenheit (15 million degrees Celsius).

- Approximately 1 million planet Earths would fit into the Sun.

- It would take a jet plane roughly 6 months to travel all the way around the Sun.

- The Sun is the largest object within our solar system.

- It comprises of 99.8% of the solar systems mass.

- The Sun's magnetic field spreads throughout the solar system via the solar wind.

- Its gravity holds the solar system together, which keeps everything from the smallest particles to the biggest planets in its orbit.

- The Sun is one star amongst billions of other stars in the Milky Way Galaxy.

- The Sun's energy gives us light and warmth and without it, life on earth would simply cease to exist.

- However, it is also extremely dangerous and could wipe us out with very little effort if conditions on the Sun changed.

Although Eugene Parker was initially criticised, afterwards he was revered by NASA, they named their space probe to the Sun – 'The Parker Space Probe.'

One of the primary reasons the Parker Space Probe was sent to the Sun was because on 1st September 1859, there was a massive explosion on the Sun!

This blast was observed by the British astronomer Richard Carrington.

Roughly 18 hours later, the shit hit the fan on Earth!

Compasses moved around and telegraph wires caught fire and broke. What happened is known as a geomagnetic storm.

The Northern Lights can be seen around the Arctic Circle.

But with this geomagnetic storm, the solar winds' charged particles hit the Earth's magnetic field and the Northern

Lights were seen as far down as Cuba.

The storm knocked out the telegraph poles for roughly 4 days. Although it may not seem like a big thing, if that were to happen today it could potentially knock out all of our electronic kit we take for granted.

Because it was Carrington who first observed this before it knocked out a lot of the communications around the world, they called it a 'Carrington Level Event.'

If a Carrington Level event happened today, many of the communication systems would be disabled. This would affect food supply chains to our homes and be disastrous to our hospital systems.

So what was the principal reason for the probe being sent up and getting so close to the Sun?

It was simply to get the data that we needed in case a Carrington Level Event happens again so we can reduce the damage that it can cause on Earth.

Depending on the size of the solar storm, only so much can be done.

However, by knowing that trouble will head to Earth in several hours, we can avoid not only billions of dollars worth of loss in industry but also reduce the loss of human life.

Just as your TV weather girl or weatherman would predict your local weather, NASA predicts the weather in space. It had been a dream for roughly 50 years to send a probe to the Sun and until recently, the technology simply wasn't there to achieve this.

On the 12th of August 2018, the Parker Solar Probe lifted off on its mission to the Sun.

As it approached the Sun, it hit speeds of a phenomenal 68,000 miles an hour.

Of course, it is very hard to comprehend that sort of speed. Just to put that in Earth terms, if you are travelling from New York to Los Angeles you will get to L.A in about 2.5 minutes at that pace.

At the front of the probe is a heat shield which comprises a ceramic coating and a type of carbon composite that gets hit by temperatures of around 1400°C.

This keeps the main body of the probe at a temperature of roughly 30°C so it can work perfectly and send data back to Earth.

The mission cost 1.5 billion dollars.

On the 1st of November 2018, the Parker Solar Probe reached speeds of 179,000 miles an hour and it became the fastest object in history made by a human.

People thought Parker was talking rubbish, but they were wrong.

Just because somebody doesn't believe in you, and thinks you're a fool, it doesn't mean they are correct.

So what can we learn from the story that we can apply to our own lives?

- Have big goals.

- Plan things out.

- It takes time and patience to reach objectives.

- Don't worry if you're criticised.

- Have the right team around you.

- Assess the risks so you can limit the risks to yourself.

- Take massive action.

- And put on your rhino skin and stand firm when people don't believe you.

CHAPTER 12

NO ONE IS BETTER THAN YOU

"If you believe in yourself and have a dedication and pride and never quit, you'll be a winner. The price of victory is high but so are the rewards."
– Bear Bryant

In the award-winning movie – 'The Kings Speech,' it shows how King George VI was wrestling with his speech impediment.

The person given the task of helping the King to overcome his stammer was Lionel Logue.

Lionel was an Australian speech and language therapist and also did some stage acting.

At the start of one scene, the King is accusing Lionel of not having the right qualifications to coach him.

This is followed by a fantastic scene where the King has his back turned to Lionel and is telling Lionel about how disappointed he is with him.

When the King turns around to look at Lionel, to his horror, he sees Lionel sitting on a chair that is only meant for King's and Queen's to sit on.

"GET UP, YOU CAN'T SIT THERE, GET UP!"

Lionel isn't bothered by what the King said and carries on sitting there. He calmly replies, "Why not? It's a chair."

The King tells him it's not just a chair and says words to the affect of, "It's Saint Edward's chair. And only a King or Queen may sit in that chair."

Lionel remains as cool as a cucumber. He isn't impressed with the 'so-called' importance of the chair.

The King, (still losing his shit) over the situation, accuses Lionel of trivialising everything.

As the King keeps on talking in his rage, he goes from stammering to talking normally. Lionel mainly did this to spark an emotion in the King and show him he could talk without his speech impediment.

If you want to see the scene on YouTube, simply type in 'Kings Speech – I Have a Voice (the channel name is 'dnasewell')

One of the brilliant things Lionel did was he challenged the King's authority and refused to be seen as inferior to anyone.

To someone with a closed mindset, they would hate it if you didn't kiss ass to a member of the Royal Family.

I'm not saying that anybody should be disrespectful to the person in authority. They should be treated as everybody should be treated.

With kindness and respect, no matter how high or how low somebody is on the social ladder.

If you want to be comfortable in your own skin, you must realise that there are no higher importance levels than you. These levels are perceptions created by others.

In reality, as a human being, nobody is above you and nobody is below you.

I've seen it many times, when people change in front of someone with a higher or lower social status than them.

When I decided to write books, I looked at how qualified I was to become an author.

I didn't do well in school, I had no background in writing, I couldn't type 100 words per minute and who am I to write a book?

These sorts of questions go through all our minds when

we decide to start something we've never done before. But to make progress we must be bold and take risks. We have to take that leap.

That's the way I've done lots of things in my life, and that's how I've achieved some things that I could have only dreamed about as a boy.

One thing I don't do is put people on too much of a pedestal.

When I had low self-esteem and low confidence, I did used to look at people as more special than me.

But now I'm comfortable with who I am and what I've done, I don't look at people that way anymore. Even though I do respect people who have made a positive difference in other peoples lives; as long as they're also kind and down-to-earth.

I see people look upon celebrities as they are some kind of Godly figure.

While it's ok to admire and respect people, remember that you are just as special as anyone else in this world.

You don't need 50 million followers on social media to be important. You don't even need to be on social media to be important.

Many people get all bent out of shape when they meet someone well known or someone who has achieved a lot.

The best thing to do when you meet someone you respect is just be yourself and act naturally.

Paul McCartney is about as high as you can get for achieving in the world of entertainment, but he's also just another guy and no better than you or me.

Paul can write, sing, and play instruments better than I ever will. However, I'm sure I could beat him on a 50-mile run and I'm sure you're better than him at certain things.

There will be things I'm better than you at, and there will be things you're better than me at.

So we are all superior and inferior to other people at different things, but ultimately, no one is better than you!

You are unique, and you have talent that only you can bring to this world.

That individual talent you have can make a difference in people's lives and your own!

And when you make a positive difference in people's lives, you become a more valuable person.

When you become a more valuable person to others and to yourself, more opportunities come your way and the better your life will be.

So never forget how important you are.

You are strong, you're unique, and you're special in ways that many people can only dream of!

CHAPTER 13

THE WELSH WARRIOR

"You develop a thick skin and you develop a certain kind of wit to defend yourself."
– Vigo Mortensen

Rhino Skin

When achieving big things in life, if you've got rhino skin, then you can make the impossible possible!

You're about to read about a man that took on overwhelming opposition. And he became a man that shone a light and lead the way for a better health care system for many people all over the world!

In the 19th century, people were making efforts to make health for individuals better in Great Britain.

Health departments were created, and slum clearances were organised, as well as improved sanitation projects. This brought an end to epidemics, such as Typhus and Cholera. Even Smallpox, one of the planet's biggest killers had reduced greatly!

When people volunteered for the Boer War in 1899, many were rejected for being underweight, too small, and not strong enough to fight. The health of men, women and children in Great Britain was not good!

In 1900, the infant mortality rate was approximately 15% and 1 out of every 200 mothers would also die in childbirth.

Also, in 1929, the Wall Street Crash happened, and the Great Depression followed. The increase in unemployment meant it was far harder for the British population to get medical care because they simply didn't have the money.

In the beginning of the 19th century, the town of Tredegar in Monmouthshire had a population of just over 1,000 people. Fortunately, iron ore deposits were discovered, and the town prospered. Most people in the town were working for the Tredegar Iron Company and production also turned to steel and coal.

However, as production would fluctuate, full-time employment would vary too.

Living conditions were very cramped back then, and it was common to have a two-bedroom house with 6 to 12 people living in it.

Also, most of the houses didn't have running water and had outside toilets.

There was no National Health System so the Tredegar Iron

& Coal Company, unlike most companies in the U.K. set up medical care for their workers, and for the workers wives and children. In return, workers would pay the company between 2 to 3 pence per pound for their medical contributions.

By the 1920s, there were 24,000 people in Tredegar and out of that number, 22,000 people in the town were members of this medical scheme. This was ground-breaking, and it would soon inspire big changes in the British medical system!

Aneurin 'Nye' Bevan was born in Tredegar in 1897 and left school to work in a coal mine at 13. He watched his father die of pneumoconiosis – a disease of the lungs caused by breathing in coal dust. This disease killed thousands of miners every year.

He'd also seen many of his colleagues lose limbs and suffer broken bones while working underground in dangerous conditions. Nye became a man of the people and entered local union politics while in his teens.

He disliked the rich having their medical needs cared for while the working class struggled to get proper medical care.

When the local Tredegar Council set up a basic local

health service, Bevan used it as a template to formulate his plan for a National Health Service.

Today, the National Health Service (NHS) is so vital, the UK cannot function without it, or should I say it wouldn't want to function without it!

At the time of writing, the NHS has never been more needed and appreciated as the COVID-19 pandemic sweeps across the planet.

The parliamentary bill to create the National Health Service was said to be one of the most fiercely contested bills in British political history. And the Tory party, led by Winston Churchill fiercely fought the bill and did everything they could to stop it being passed!

Churchill believed that having a National Health Service was too expensive and too complex to achieve for a country in such a financial mess after World War II.

This was a bold move by Bevan!

Most people would have buckled as soon as a powerhouse like Churchill declared his opposition to the bill.

However, Bevan had rhino skin and would take on anyone regardless of who they were or what they had achieved!

Nothing like this had ever been done before, and Bevan was being attacked on all fronts.

The National Health Service was the most expensive and biggest social reform ever thought up in the U.K.

Although Churchill had done an incredible job with leading Great Britain to victory in World War II, he sometimes lacked empathy and compassion for the average person. Churchill was born into an aristocratic family; whose ancestral home was Blenheim Palace.

He also felt threatened by Bevan because Bevan was one of the few people who would routinely stand up and challenge the former wartime Prime Minister.

However, despite their differing political stance, Churchill admired the sharp-witted tenacity of Bevan.

Bevan believed people should have medical freedom. So if you got sick, or anyone in your family had a life-threatening illness; you wouldn't have to worry about paying to get treatment.

In one of his speeches he said,

"Illness is neither an indulgence for which people have to pay, nor an offence for which they should be penalised, but a misfortune the cost of which should be shared by the community."

However, the British media ripped into Bevan and said that it was a disastrous decision to create free healthcare.

The vast majority of doctors, dentists and surgeons were all opposed to free health care because they believed it would affect their freedom and also their income.

Rather than looking at the big picture and how many millions of sick men, women, and children it could help, many of the medical staff were more concerned about themselves.

Many doctors said Bevan's service couldn't work because they – the doctors themselves would refuse to work and help people.

The BMA (British Medical Association) carried out a survey in 1948 and claimed that only 4,734 doctors out of the 45,148 polled were in favour of a National Health Service.

To say that Aneurin Bevan was up against it was a massive understatement!

Before the NHS come along Great Britain's health was in

poor shape. 1947 was a bitterly cold winter, and is one of the coldest winters on record. London's River Thames froze over, and it snowed heavily.

Many British people couldn't afford heating which meant they were far more likely to become ill.

Millions of British people would go untreated because they couldn't afford healthcare. They wouldn't go to doctors, dentists or opticians, because they simply didn't have the money.

However, as much as there were people who were against the NHS, there were also millions of people desperate to have the service.

One of Bevan's friends – Jeffrey Goodman, who was a journalist said,

"In my Father's Day in the 1930s people had to suffer when there was no such thing as a health service. If you came from the working class, the problems of falling ill were a nightmare for all working-class families!"

Between the First World War and the Second World War there was a lot of scarlet fever, diphtheria, and measles.

Thousands of people died every year from tuberculosis

because of the lack of medical care. And if a child was lucky enough to make it to age 12, the chances were that he or she had a weak heart, rotten teeth, and poor bones.

There was also a very high mortality rate with babies, and the nurses spent a lot of their mornings writing death certificates.

Back then in the suburbs of England there was one doctor per 250 people but in London there was only one doctor for every 18,000 people!

The healthcare was run more like a charity where people would try to raise money to get themselves or their families seen to.

Many rich people gave sizeable sums of cash to the charities, but what they gave wasn't enough. There needed to be a better system put in place.

When the soldiers returned to Great Britain after the war, Bevan believed they deserved a free health service after what they had done for their country.

Bevan also guaranteed the doctors that he would equal their pay or if they felt they weren't getting enough money; they could still practice with private clients on the side.

He always believed that there had to be a better way of organising things for medical healthcare.

In one of Bevan speeches he said:

"There is a school of thought that if a thing is scarce, that it ought to be dear. Although it doesn't cost any more to produce it, than if it were plentiful. Now that's alright from the point of view of orthodox economics, but this isn't an orthodox government and I'm not an orthodox minister of health."

This was part of Bevan's brilliance!

He didn't follow the crowd, and he didn't think that just because things are done in a certain way, things should remain unchanged. Bevan challenged the normal way, and he always wanted to make things better for people.

This falls right in line with all the extensive research I have done on some of history's greatest inventors. They're always looking to improve things for people. And when you improve things for other people... your own life will improve.

When Bevan announced that everybody in Great Britain would have free healthcare based on people's individual ability to pay (which was taken from their taxes) on 3

January 1948, it was an enormous task and many people felt that Bevan couldn't pull through with this promise.

Bevan had only six months to set up Great Britain's biggest ever social reform.

He wanted to change the way society did things, and to say this task was against the odds would be an understatement!

How many times have we heard politicians say that they will do things and never follow through with their promises?

But Bevan was a different kettle of fish and he was relentless with the task in hand. He put all of his energy into it and was constantly thinking about his fellow man and woman.

Bevan had to think of ways to recruit all the staff needed for the hospitals. He had to find which buildings were going to be the hospitals and if there weren't enough hospitals, then more needed to be built.

He had to find all the machines that the hospital used, and all the pharmaceutical drugs. And when doctors and the nurses and the rest of the staff were in place, he needed to find managers that could run the hospitals and know how much money to give each hospital.

Despite his good intentions, the committee of the British Medical Association were relentless in their attack of Bevan.

These were some of the smartest minds around the country, but the smartest of all of them was a man called Dr Charles Hill. Hill was not only very smart but also quick witted!

Hill was a master of persuasion and was also the most famous doctor in the country. He spoke on BBC TV every week to over 14 million people and gave them medical advice.

So Bevan had seriously tough opposition! Not only with Winston Churchill but also in Dr Charles Hill!

If Bevan was to beat these two brilliant men, he would need the thickest rhino mental armour that you can possibly imagine!

Mail was sent out to thousands of doctors to persuade them not to join Bevan's NHS. They sent out letters saying things such as,

"We should not be governed by an ex coal miner!"

They also said that this was the beginning of turning Great Britain into a socialist economy and the British medical Association compared Bevan to Hitler. There was a lot of snobbery with many doctors, and they tried to look down at Bevan because of his humble beginnings.

However, they didn't realise that Bevan had the toughest of rhino skins and how relentless he was!

And because somebody starts off in a lower class in society doesn't mean that they can't achieve great things.

Bevan believed in health care for his country so much that he was willing to give his life for it if need be.

Although the vast majority of the British Medical Association was against the NHS, there were many young medical people who could see sense in Bevan's plans.

Many of the older, more set in their ways doctors branded the young medics as traitors.

Some medical students were called a commie bastard for wanting a National Health Service.

When over 85% of the medical profession voted against joining the NHS, this was an enormous setback to Bevan's plans and defeat to Bevan looked imminent.

After this vote, most of the medical team sat there like a bunch of smug bastards! They felt that victory was now inevitable.

However, they didn't realise they were dealing with a crazy coal mining rhinoceros that would charge forward, deflect all criticism, and smash through any setbacks in his path!

Bevan wasn't just critical towards many of the Conservative party's decisions. He was also very critical about his own Labour leadership decisions.

He didn't blindly follow what his party wanted him to follow. He was his own man and spoke his own mind.

Bevan didn't care if what he said stopped his promotion or got him sacked.

He always followed his heart and believed what he was doing was the right thing for people.

Bevan loved and believed in Abraham Lincoln's quote:

"Government of the people, by the people, for the people, shall not perish from the earth."

I had seen Bevan's statue many times in Cardiff before,

but it wasn't until I learned more about the great man that I truly understood what an incredible person he was.

Gallup published a public opinion poll about the NHS. Even though most of the doctors were against the service, most of the public supported it. Only 13% of the public were behind the doctors.

Because of the overwhelming public support, Bevan decided there was no point in talking to many of the top GP's (General practitioners) that had rejected his plans.

He decided to go right to Britain's top doctor... Lord Moran who was the President of the Royal College of Physicians.

This was an interesting move, as Lord Moran was Winston Churchill's personal doctor and of course Churchill wasn't a fan of Bevan's NHS.

In other words, Bevan walked right into the wolves' den with the top wolf!

But Bevan didn't give two fucks!

Why?

Because a 5,000-pound rhino doesn't fear a 110-pound wolf!

With that said, Moran was a very clever man and amazingly, these two men didn't clash. Moran respected Bevan for his intelligence and what he was trying to do for the British public.

Lord Moran was in charge of the country's most prestigious medical group - the consultants.

Even though the consultants were highly against the NHS, they were also in charge of many of London's charity hospitals such as Saint Thomas's and the London hospital.

Bevan knew that there was something that the consultants wanted and that was more money for the charity hospitals.

Even though there were doctors that were more concerned about their own personal finances than the health of the nation as a whole, there were also many doctors that wanted to do everything they could to help the average family.

Although the charity hospitals were running, they didn't have much cash, and they needed more.

Bevan's plan of action was to give the doctors and the consultants as much individual freedom as they desired. He also wanted to create a way of getting more funds to the consultant's charity hospitals.

One of the things that many people do when they have an opposite opinion to somebody else is they will just keep clashing and saying things like, "I'm right to do it this way, and you're wrong!"

That's one way to do things, and sometimes it will work. However, if you do it in a harsh worded manner, then the other person is going to feel scolded, and possibly humiliated.

One of the most effective things I found when trying to get a good outcome from the other person is to think about where the other person is coming from. And Bevan was a master of this!

It may sound bizarre to try to find a way of helping your so-called enemy, but by doing this, it is possible to bring them around to your way of thinking.

Bevan did something here that I have used into my own life to great effect, and those two things are:

1. Go to the top person if you can get to them.

2. Try to find a way to help the other person and come to an agreement, which can benefit both parties.

However, even if Lord Moran would come on his side,

one of Moran's opponents was Lord Horder, who was the King's physician.

Unfortunately for Bevan, Horder had come from a very privileged background and was massively against the National Health Service!

If Lord Moran couldn't get more support than Lord Horder, then there was a great chance that Bevan's plans of launching the NHS would be dashed.

Moran had always beat Horder in the past in the election to become the President of the Royal College of Physicians.

But this time Horder was promoting his anti NHS policy. And at the time, most people believed doctors would vote for Horder and not Moran.

This was not only a vote for the presidency, but it was also a vote to establish whether the NHS would begin or not.

In the end, when it came down to the doctor's votes, it was close... seriously close!

As 165 doctors voted for Horder and 170 voted for Moran.

There was only one thing to do now, and that was to convince the GP's that Bevan's NHS wouldn't make them all work for the state and take away their independence.

Bevan made another clever move! He amended the NHS proposal where all doctors could have their independence and not ever be in a position to have to work for the state full time.

However, just as the wise Welsh Rhino thought he was going to have his breakthrough, many doctors threatened to strike if the NHS was going to become a reality.

This move would've been disastrous, not only for the creation of the NHS, but also for the health of the British people who needed to see doctors.

The rejection and the resistance from the doctors was relentless, but so was Bevan's will.

At this point, Aneurin Bevan made one of the boldest moves in British political history.

Even though there were no doctors on board, Bevan launched a campaign saying that the NHS was going to start on 5th July.

Many doctors thought this was ludicrous, but Bevan had unbelievable faith in himself and he believed that somehow he would pull it off.

Bevan's plan of action was to build up a campaign so strong that the doctors would look like complete c***s if they went on strike and didn't help anybody that was sick or dying.

And when Bevan launched the first public campaign, over 20 million people signed up for the service.

Bevan made another clever decision that outflanked even the great Sir Winston Churchill.

Aneurin Bevan targeted the adverts towards women and children. This move was pure genius!

In the past, unless they were rich, many women in the U.K. would come in second when it came to medical care.

As for the children back then, thousands of children were dying from diphtheria alone!

Diphtheria was a particularly nasty disease, which was caused by a germ in the throat and produced a poison that would end up attacking the body.

Sometimes when the windpipe was affected, the patient would be choked and die from asphyxiation.

Diphtheria was a major cause of illness and death among

children. It was all over the world. In the United States, their worst year was 1921, which produced 206,000 cases, which resulted in 15,520 deaths in that one year!

Because the way the health care system was at the time, you were only guaranteed medical care if you were well off or rich.

Thousands upon thousands of working-class parents' children were dying when they just didn't need to die!

In the case of diphtheria, all they needed was immunisation. But the reason so many of them were dying from diphtheria was because many of the working-class families simply couldn't afford it.

However, with new NHS system people wouldn't have to pay for it directly and this was hugely appealing to families.

And there is nothing, but nothing a loving parent won't protect more than their child!

Most parents would do whatever is necessary to protect their own children, so Bevan's campaign appealed to most of the public.

Within a few short weeks over 75% of the British public

signed up for the NHS.

The British Medical Association who were opposed to the NHS were now starting to look like a bunch of selfish fools. At this point, almost half of the doctors changed their minds and wanted to be a part of the NHS.

With only five weeks to go before the launch of the National Health Service, the British Medical Association advised all the doctors to join the NHS.

Even though the BMA agreed to join the NHS, they wanted Bevan to push back the deadline of 5th July because they believed that it may weaken his stand with the NHS and there was still an opportunity to turn things around.

Other people in the BMA believed that it was unrealistic to get everything ready by 5th July, but Bevan charged forward. He decided if he pushed back the date by six months, it would be a sign of him showing weakness!

Bevan knew that the launch on 5th July wouldn't be perfect, but he believed that it would be better to launch without a perfect system than not to launch at all. He knew if they made a start, they could build upon what they had created.

Aneurin Bevan knew that they needed huge amount of funds for the NHS, but as large as the funds would be, they would still not be as much as the funds that were supplied for the military.

When World War II was raging and the blitz hit London, most of the hospitals were damaged, which meant most of the hospitals had to be rebuilt.

So how would Bevan find the money from an already financially struggling Britain after World War II?

With less than five weeks to go, Bevan had a massive shortage of not only the buildings that he needed, but of nurses.

He needed to find 30,000 nurses to look after roughly 400,000 hospital beds.

A huge campaign went out looking for new nurses. If they weren't already qualified nurses, then they needed to be trained as soon as possible.

Bevan was also being smashed by the media, who predicted that a free health service would turn most of the population into freebie seekers that would no longer work, and no longer contribute towards society.

The media predicted that the entire NHS system would collapse, but it never happened.

On 5th July 1948, Aneurin Bevan's rhino skin and relentlessness paid off!

The British people now had access to a healthcare service for all and didn't have to worry about if they could afford it.

On the first day the NHS was born, Aneurin Bevan visited Manchester Trafford Park Hospital.

When Bevan turned up in Manchester people were in awe of him and what he and his team had achieved.

But Bevan was down-to-earth and always treated people as he wanted to be treated.

There wasn't a pompous, 'look how amazing I am' attitude.

Bevan was a man that followed his heart and did what was right for the British people. By doing that, he changed history!

Aneurin Bevan's rhino skin and determination have saved more British lives than you can shake a stick at.

Infant mortality halved within the first 10 years of the NHS!

People dying from infectious diseases dropped by over 80%!

And

Life expectancy increased!

People can argue all day long about the good points of something and the bad points of the NHS, which is fine.

However, in large, the NHS focused solely on helping the people, and the British people are extremely lucky to have it.

American Katherine Zaleski, who is (at the time of writing) the senior writer for the Huffington Post fell ill in the UK and couldn't believe the level of care she received from the NHS.

Katherine said:

"It was amazing, I thought I would have to pay a huge amount of money and I basically just walked into a National Health office. I met with the doctor immediately and we sat together for 30 minutes, he gave me a prescription, I walked downstairs, and I didn't have to pay a cent."

Katherine went on to say that of course it doesn't cover every single type of specialised care immediately, but in terms of basic care and service, the UK is way beyond most of the countries in the world!

Experts from the Commonwealth Fund rated the NHS system as the safest and most affordable health care system out of the 11 wealthy countries it looked at.

The other leading countries were:
2nd Australia.
3rd The Netherlands.
4th Norway.
5th New Zealand.
The NHS was revolutionary!

It became the world's first health care system, which was not based on insurance premiums or individual payments.

People in the U.K. also have the choice to pay for private medical care outside of the NHS if they wish to.

Aneurin Bevan was up against some colossal challenges and some enormously powerful people.

There was immense pressure on Bevan and most people would've cracked under the strain.

However, by having rhino skin and holding onto his dream, he achieved something phenomenal.

Aneurin Bevan stood strong and became one of the greatest rhinos that Great Britain has ever produced!

So, if the son of a poor coal miner can achieve great things against phenomenal odds, then surely with a big dream, massive action, determination, and rhino skin we too can achieve great things in our own lives.

So, go out there, put on your RHINO SKIN, CHARGE FORWARD and kick ass in the game of life!

ACKNOWLEDGEMENTS

It's almost impossible to say how many people have helped me along the way with producing this book, and if you're not in the acknowledgements just know that I am very grateful for your support and help.

However, I would like to say a massive THANK YOU to a few people that I can think of, off the top of my head:

My Mum – Diana Beckerleg, 29 Commando Regiment, Royal Artillery, 3 Commando Brigade and The British Army.

Tom Webb, Paul 'The Viking' Hughes, Thomas Hughes, Eva Savage, Mark 'Billy' Billingham, Julie Colombino-Billingham, Tracy, Maria and Kay Morris, Cheryl Hicks, Jamie Baulch, Gene Hipgrave, Kauri-Romet Aadamsoo, Mark Dawson, Craig Martelle, Michael Anderle, James Blatch, Michael and Emma Byrne, Paul 'Faz' Farrington, Des BlackWood, Paul Heaney, James Atkinson, Des Powell and Laura Taylor.

Also, a huge THANKS to 'The Mark Llewhellin Advance Reader Team' for taking the time to read the manuscript and make suggestions.

ABOUT THE AUTHOR

In 1990, Mark Llewhellin left school without knowing his grades. He had little confidence and was not at all optimistic about his future.

Not knowing what to do with his life Mark followed some of his friends into the Army. He failed his basic 1.5-mile run, was bullied, and was also voted the fattest person in the Troop!

After a year with the Junior Leaders Regiment Royal Artillery, Mark decided he would try and get into 29 Commando Regiment Royal Artillery, which is an elite Army Commando Regiment that at the time proudly held the Military Marathon World Record (i.e. a marathon carrying a 40lbs backpack).

After failing the 29 Commando Selection phase (called 'The Beat Up') twice, first through lack of fitness and secondly through an injury, Mark subsequently passed on his third attempt and completed the 'All Arms Commando Course' on his first attempt.

Mark later went on to achieve the following:

- Break the 100-kilometre Treadmill World Record.

- Place 1st in the Strava Distance Challenge in 2015 competing against over 51,000 runners.

- Place 1st in the Strava Distance Challenge in 2014 competing against over 40,000 runners.

- Run and walk 70-miles without training on his 40th birthday.

- Become a successful Personal Fitness Trainer.

- Complete the Marathon Des Sables (a six-day, 135-mile ultra-marathon in the Sahara Desert).

- Work and live in London's exclusive Park Lane as a Bodyguard.

- Run 1,620 miles in the United States whilst carrying a 35lbs pack.

Mark has interviewed some of the world's top performers and high achievers in various locations, including one of the world's most prestigious memorabilia rooms…the Hard Rock Café Vault Room in London.

He has travelled to over 50 countries and has been featured in leading national newspapers and on TV for his running achievements.

Mark has extensively worked in the support and care industry for many years helping individuals with brain injury, autism, epilepsy, dyspraxia, and various types of learning difficulties.

He is the Managing Director of Mark 7 Productions, as well as the Producer and Host of 'An Audience with Mark Billy Billingham' speaking events around the UK.

Mark is currently working on more personal development books and lives with his son Léon (when Léon's not at his Mum's) on a beautiful marina in South West Wales.

ALSO BY MARK LLEWHELLIN

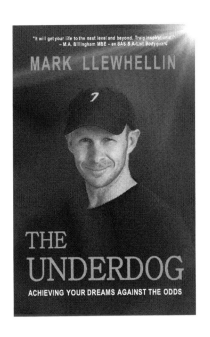

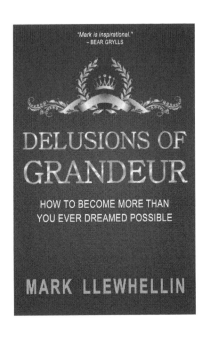

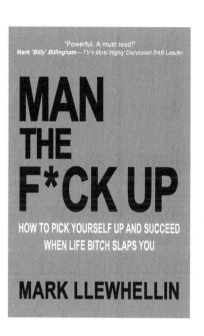

GET TWO FREE MARK LLEWHELLIN BOOKS AND DEALS AND UPDATES

Join 'The Mark Llewhellin Advance Reader Team' for information on new books and deals plus:

You can pick up FREE copies of Mark's five star reviewed books:

1. 'The Underdog'

2. 'Delusions of Grandeur'

Simply go to Mark's website at www.markllewhellin.com and sign up for FREE.

REFERENCES

National Geographic's Mission to the Sun
Oxford Dictionary
PBS – Einstein's Big Idea
Potter Next Chapter
Hunker
Simon Whistler
Biographics
BBC – The NHS: Difficult Beginning
Wikipedia
Imelda Staunton
Ian MacMillan
Mark Hayhurst
Charlotte Moore
Edmund Coulthard
Grant McKee
David Byrne
YouTube
Spartacus Educational
On Other Issues
Jesse Gordon
The Guardian
BBC
Health Before The NHS 1 The Road To Recovery
The British Journal of Nursing
History of Vaccines
Listverse
J Frater
ABC Network
EldoradoTrading
Forbes
Skavlan
The Hollywood Masters – Netflix

DISCLAIMER

Although the author and publisher have made every effort to ensure that the information contained in this book was accurate at the time of release, the author and publisher do not assume and hereby disclaim any liability to any party for any loss, damage, or disruption caused by errors or omissions in this book, whether such errors or omissions result from negligence, accident, or any other cause.

A Mark 7 Publications Paperback.

First published in Great Britain in 2021

by Mark 7 Publications

ISBN 978-1-914006-10-4

Book design and formatting by Tom Webb
pixelfiddler@hotmail.co.uk

IF YOU ENJOYED THIS BOOK

Your help in spreading the word about Mark's books is greatly appreciated and your reviews make a huge difference to help new readers change their lives for the better.

If you found this book useful please leave a review on the platform you purchased it on.

Live Your Dreams!

Mark